Contents

Xavi Hernández

THE PASS MASTER

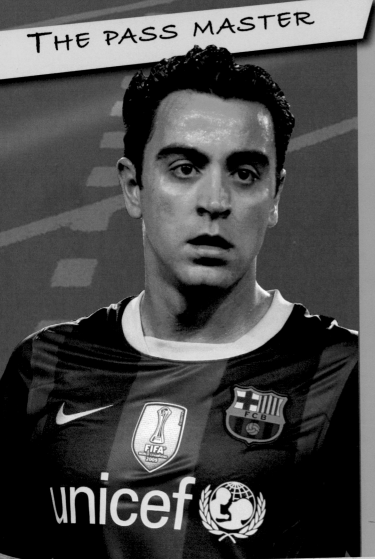

Xavi Hernández during a Spanish league match between FC Barcelona and Sporting Gijon at Nou Camp Stadium.

Xavi Hernández's all-time favourite player is Manchester United's retired midfielder Paul Scholes.

Stats!

Name: Xavier Hernández i Creus

Date of birth: 25 January 1980

Place of birth: Terrassa, Spain

Sport Football

Teams: FC Barcelona (1998-present), Spain (2000-present)

Early days: Hernández joined Barcelona's legendary La Masia training academy at 11 years old. He progressed through the youth and reserve teams, and helped the Barcelona B team win promotion to the Spanish Second Division. He made his first team debut in 1998, when star midfielder (now Barcelona manager) Pep Guardiola was out of the team injured, and has been a regular ever since.

Major achievements: Hernández holds Barcelona's all-time appearance record. He has also won three Champions League titles (2006, 2009, 2011), and seven Spanish league titles (1998-99, 2004-05, 2005-06, 2008-09, 2009-10, 2010-11, 2012-13). He won the European Championship with Spain in 2008 and 2012, and the World Cup in 2010. He was voted Player of the Tournament at Euro 2008.

Secrets of success: Hernández's skill is finding time and space to pass the ball to his teammates. Hernández is the master of the perfectly delivered pass, a feat that he makes look easy!

Life Story

A fanatical Barcelona supporter, Hernández's childhood bedroom was filled with team scarves, hats, and anything else he could find. But the football-mad youngster never thought he would be good enough to play for his idols. Every year, Barcelona held youth trials but Hernández never dared attend. One year, though, word of his abilities reached the club's coaches and he received an official invite to come along. The rest, as they say, is history.

Hernández perfected his skills at Barcelona's youth training academy, where every player is taught the values of hard work, teamwork and ball control. He has played alongside many of the same teammates – for Barcelona and for Spain – since he was a boy, and almost telepathically knows when and where to pass the ball to create goal-scoring opportunities.

Xavi in action during a Spanish League match between FC Barcelona and Real Sociedad in Barcelona, 12 December 2010.

Like other world-class sportsmen and women, Hernández is able to perform at the very highest levels when it matters the most – in the big games, where trophies are won and history books are written. In the 2011 Champions League final against Manchester United, he ran further than anyone else on the pitch and passed the ball more often than Manchester United's three midfield players *put together*!

Questions and Answers

Q What's the secret of your passing success?

'I spend the entire 90 minutes looking for space on the pitch. I'm always thinking, 'The defence is *here* so I get the ball and I go *there* to where the space is.'

Xavi Hernández, *Daily Mail*, 2011

Q Barcelona are considered the best team in the world. Why are they so good?

'Some youth academies worry about winning, we worry about education. The first thing they teach you is think, think, think. Lift your head up. Look before you get the ball... Play the ball first time. Modern football is so quick that two touches means too slow.'

Xavi Hernández, *The Guardian*, 2011

Usain Bolt

LIGHTNING BOLT

Usain Bolt celebrates his 100 metres world record victory during the 2008 Beijing Olympics, China.

Usain Bolt's favourite pre-race meal is chicken nuggets!

Stats!

Name: Usain St Leo Bolt

Date of birth: 21 August 1986

Place of birth: Trelawny, Jamaica

Sport: Athletics

Teams: N/A

Early days: In 2002, aged only 15, Bolt won the Jamaican high school titles in the 200m and 400m, and became the youngest junior champion in history – competing against athletes up to four years older than himself. In 2003 and 2004 he set junior world records for the 200m, and was the first junior to break 20 seconds for the 200m.

Major achievements: Bolt won gold medals in the 100m and 200m at the 2008 Beijing Olympics, both in world record times. He also won Gold in the men's 4 x 100m relay. He followed this with gold medals in the same events at the 2012 London Olympics, and is also the reigning World champion at the 100m and the men's 4 x 100m relay.

Secrets of success: Experts put Bolt's success down to his height. At 6' 5" he is very tall for a sprinter, and starts slowly but his long legs mean he takes just 41 strides to complete 100m – his competitors take between 45 and 48!

Life Story

The fastest man on earth could easily have become a cricketer instead of a sprinter. Bolt's father was a cricket fanatic, and as a child Bolt was a talented fast bowler. By the time he had reached senior school, however, athletics coaches had noticed his speed, and had him training for the 200m and 400m.

Questions and Answers

Q How much of your speed is natural?

'I could run under 10 seconds now even if I didn't really train, but to win medals it's all about training on the track, working in the gym, and improving my technique.'

Usain Bolt, *Shortlist*, 2011

Q You never look stressed before a race. Why is that?

'Before the Junior World Championships [at 15] I was so nervous I put my shoes on the wrong feet! I was shaking because everybody was expecting me to win... That one moment changed my whole life, because after that I was like, why should I worry? Now I just try to relax.'

Usain Bolt, *The Guardian*, 2010

Usain is triumphant as he wins the Men's 200m Final in Beijing, 2008.

The young Bolt excelled and quickly started winning national and international titles at 200m and 400m. But he had his heart set on running the 100m. Coaches told him he was too tall – most sprinters are around six foot – but Bolt made a deal: 'If I break the Jamaican record for the 200m, you'll let me run the 100m'. In 2007, he ran 19.75 seconds, breaking a record that had stood for 36 years. Bolt's 100m career had begun.

In the Beijing Olympics in 2008, Bolt stunned the world with record times in the 100m and 200m. In the 100m final he ran 9.69 seconds, not only visibly slowing down towards the end of the race to celebrate victory, but also running with one shoelace undone.

Jessica Ennis

GOLDEN GIRL

Jessica Ennis celebrates winning the women's 60m Hurdles on 29 January 2011 in Scotland.

Jessica Ennis won £22,000 for finishing first at the 2009 World Championships – but didn't pick up her prize money for three months!

Life Story

When Jessica Ennis's parents enrolled her at athletics camp in the summer of 1996, they were just trying to find something to fill the long school holidays. Instead, they started their daughter on the path to becoming a world – and Olympic – champion!

Ennis won her first athletics prize that summer at Sheffield's Don Valley Stadium – a pair of trainers. Most importantly, though, she discovered skills that would turn her into a world beater. At 11, she joined City of Sheffield Athletic Club and rose steadily through the junior and senior ranks, all the while showing signs of the potential that would take her to the top of her sport.

In the 2006 Commonwealth Games she won a bronze medal, but her heptathlon high jump was so good, it would have won a Gold in the individual high jump event had she entered it.

Jessica Ennis competing during the women's heptathlon high jump at the 2010 European Athletics Championships in Barcelona.

Questions and Answers

Q Are you happy with what you've achieved so far?

A 'As an athlete you're never happy! Even if you won the Olympics and got the world record I think you'd still be like, 'Why didn't I run a little bit faster in the hurdles or jump a little bit higher?' You always want a little bit more. That's what keeps you moving forward.'

Jessica Ennis, *The Mirror*, 2011

Q Do you enjoy being labelled Britain's Golden Girl?

A 'Being expected to win every time I compete in a heptathlon does bring a lot of pressure. But at the same time it motivates me, pushes me on and makes me want to step up my game.'

Jessica Ennis, *The Mirror*, 2011

Mao Asada

THE ICE QUEEN

Japanese figure skater Mao Asada poses for photographs in Nagoya, Japan, wearing a kimono from her own designer clothes line.

Mao Asada holds a Guinness World Record for the most triple-axel jumps performed in one competition.

Stats!

Name: Mao Asada

Date of birth: 25 September 1990

Place of birth: Nagoya, Japan

Sport: Figure skating

Teams: N/A

Early days: Asada started skating at five years old. She won the Japanese Novice National championships in 2002-03. In 2004-05 she won the Japanese Junior National Championships and the ISU Junior Grand Prix. She qualified for the World Junior Figure Skating Championships when she was 15.

Major achievements: Graduating to senior level, Asada has won six Japanese Championships and two World Championships. Despite qualifying for the 2006 Winter Olympics, Asada was too young to compete. She had to wait four more years for the Vancouver Games in 2010, where she won silver.

Secrets of success: Figure skating is a mixture of control, grace and fearlessness. Difficult routines take weeks of practice. Asada pushes herself to the limit!

Life Story

At 15 years old, Mao Asada had the world at her feet. She was the winner of the 2006 Grand Prix Final, the best women's figure skater in the world, the skater who everyone else had to beat. But Olympic rules meant that Asada was too young – by just 87 days – to compete in the 2006 Winter Olympics.

Questions and Answers

Q How do you manage to conquer nerves when you're competing?

A 'There are times when I don't! In the past, I used to worry about the other skaters, or other things around me, but now I mostly don't notice them. I feel very strongly that I have to get my own performance right [and everything else will follow].'

Mao Asada, http://ameblo.jp/ 2009

Q What will you do when you retire from skating?

A 'At the moment, skating is my life. But one day, I want to teach little children how to skate. I will definitely stay involved with the sport.'

Mao Asada, http://ameblo.jp/ 2009

She sat out the competition and vowed to come back better than ever. Just two months after the Olympics, Asada became the first woman to land two triple-axel jumps in the same program.

Figure skating competitors interpret music – showing judges their technical ability on the ice, and add complicated, high scoring jumps to their routines to boost their points.

Asada's triple-axel brought her two World Championship triumphs in 2008 and 2010. It also brought her disappointment. When she failed to land the jump at the 2010 Winter Olympics, she lost the gold medal to South Korean Kim Yuna. But Asada's talent made her Japan's most recognisable female celebrity. When she skates, TV audiences grow, and sponsors endorse events. Asada is the ice queen.

Mao Asada performs in the ISU World Figure Skating Championships on 30 April, 2011 in Moscow.

Sebastian Vettel

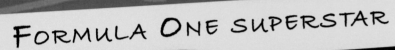

FORMULA ONE SUPERSTAR

Sebastian Vettel at the Australian Formula One Grand Prix in Albert Park, Melbourne, 28 March 2010.

If he wasn't an F1 driver, Sebastian Vettel says he would have liked to be a singer like Michael Jackson.

Stats!

Name: Sebastian Vettel

Date of birth: 3 July 1987

Place of birth: Heppenheim, Germany

Sport: Formula One racing

Teams: BMW Sauber (2006-07), Toro Rosso (2007-08), Red Bull Racing (2009-present)

Early days: Vettel started racing go-karts at three years old, winning the Junior Kart Cup in 2001. In 2004 he won the German Formula BMW Championship with an amazing 18 victories in 20 races, and was invited by the Williams racing team to help test their Formula One car.

Major achievements: His debut at the 2007 US Grand Prix made Vettel the youngest driver ever to compete in F1. He was named Rookie of the Year in 2008, and was the youngest ever championship runner-up in 2009. Vettel has won three F1 World Championships, and is on track to win his fourth title in 2013.

Secrets of success: At eight years old, Vettel was spotted by the talent scout who discovered F1 legend Michael Schumacher. He saw the same qualities in the young Vettel – stamina, fighting spirit, pride and a desire to always be the best.

Life Story

Vettel in action on the track, Petronas Formula One, Sepang circuit, Malaysia, 2 April 2010.

Sebastian Vettel's Formula One career couldn't have started more disastrously. After four races of the 2008 season, he was the only driver who had failed to finish a single race. A combination of accidents and engine failure prevented him from seeing the chequered flag, and left him rock bottom of the drivers' championship.

Vettel's self-belief was tested to the limit – and he came out on top. In Monaco he scored his first championship points, and at the Italian Grand Prix he recorded his first victory – the youngest driver ever to win an F1 race at 21 years and 73 days.

Questions and Answers

Q You started racing go-karts very young. Did you have to make sacrifices growing up?

'My parents invested a lot of money in it. We never went on holiday. When all my friends were off skiing, we were spending every weekend on the karting track. But we were having fun!'

Sebastian Vettel, *The Telegraph*, 2011

Q What does it feel like to drive an F1 car?

A 'Nothing comes close to the sensation... the forces, the power, the braking... the cornering speed. When you walk the track and see corners that you were going round at 160mph, you wonder how you could be so stupid... But in the car, you don't think like that.'

Sebastian Vettel, *The Telegraph*, 2011

The following season, Vettel switched to the Red Bull team, and has raced his way to the top of his chosen sport with barely time to check the rearview mirror. Vettel is still incredibly young, but races with the maturity of the Formula One legend, and fellow countryman, Michael Schumacher.

Vettel's skill, bravery, consistency and talent mean that fans and F1 experts alike are tipping him to dominate the sport for years to come.

David Weir

The Wheelchair Racer

David Weir shows off his gold medals at a reception for Olympic and Paralympic athletes on 10 September 2012.

David Weir's sporting idol is another David: footballer David Beckham.

Stats!

Name: David Russell Weir

Date of birth: 5 June 1979

Place of birth: Wallington, England

Sport: Wheelchair racing

Teams: N/A

Early days: Weir was a talented wheelchair athlete as a child. He represented his borough at the London Youth Games, and won the junior London Wheelchair Marathon seven times.

Major achievements: Weir has won an astonishing 10 Paralympic medals: a Silver in the 100m and a Bronze in the 200m in Athens in 2004; Golds in the 800m and 1500m, a Silver in the 400m and a Bronze in the 5000m in Beijing in 2008 and Golds in the 800m, 1500m, 5000m and the Marathon in London in 2012. He also has six World Championship gold medals, and has won the London Wheelchair Marathon six times.

Secrets of success: Weir trains hard, twice a day, six times a week, to stay at the top of his game. But his coach also attributes his success to psychology: he has the self-belief and the confidence to win races.

Life Story

David Weir was born with a damaged spinal cord, meaning he has some feeling in the lower half of his body, but he cannot stand up. As a child, he loved football and boxing, but couldn't play those sports because of a lack of wheelchair facilities. He tried wheelchair basketball, then turned to racing after watching the London Marathon wheelchair race. He entered the mini-marathon

Questions and Answers

Q **Is it ever difficult to keep motivated?**

A 'Winning keeps me going and I'm frightened of losing if I'm telling the truth. I don't want to lose my titles and my world records that I have worked so hard to get.'

David Weir, *Metro*, 2007

Q **What advice would you give other paralympic athletes?**

A 'Go and try every sport. There's enough sports out there for someone with a disability to find something they enjoy. Don't think about what you can't do, think about what you can do.'

David Weir, www.nhs.uk/Livewell, 2012

Weir racing in the men's 1500m T54 final at the International Paralympic Committee Athletics World Championships,

at the age of eight and did surprisingly well, despite having to race in his everyday wheelchair. He went on to win the race seven times.

Weir first competed at the Paralympic Games in Atlanta in 1996. He did not enjoy the experience, and took a four-year break from racing. However, fellow wheelchair athlete Tanni Grey-Thompson's success at the Sydney Paralympics inspired him to take up sport again, and he triumphed in Athens in 2004.

Tirunesh Dibaba

FAST TRACK TO SUCCESS

Tirunesh Dibaba poses with her gold medal following the Women's 10,000m race at the Beijing Olympic Games, 16 August 2008.

Tirunesh Dibaba's first name translates as 'You are good'.

Stats!

Name: Tirunesh Dibaba Kenene

Date of birth: 1 October 1985

Place of birth: Bekoji, Arsi, Ethiopia

Teams: N/A

Sport: Long distance running

Early days: At 15, Dibaba moved to the Ethiopian capital, Addis Ababa, to live with her older sister, who was training with the women's national running team. She started training alongside her sister, and was selected for the 2001 World Cross Country Championships. Competing against runners who were five and six years her senior, she finished fifth and took up running full time.

Major achievements: Dibaba won gold medals in the World Cross Country Championships in 2003, 2005, 2006 and 2008. She won gold medals in the 5,000m and 10,000m at the Beijing Olympics in 2008 – becoming the first woman ever to win both events at the same Olympics. She set a new Olympic record time for the 10,000m and the second fastest time ever. She defended her Olympic title at the 2012 Games, winning Gold in the 10,000m.

Secrets of success: Despite her slight 5" 1' (155cm) frame, Dibaba has surprising power and a great sprint finish. She frequently runs the final 400m of a race in under a minute.

Life Story

Tirunesh Dibaba was born in 1985, the year that Ethiopia's devastating famine was brought to the world's attention by Sir Bob Geldof's Live Aid concerts. To merely stay alive was a challenge; to become the best female distance runner in the world would have seemed a distant dream.

But Dibaba's family have athletics in their DNA. Her older sister Ejegayehu was an Olympic silver medallist in 2004, cousin Derartu Tulu is a double Olympic Gold medallist, and younger brother, Dejene, and sister, Genzebe, are also making their mark on the sport.

Dibaba holds the Ethiopian flag after winning the women's 10,000m race at the African Senior Athletics Championship, Nairobi, 31 July, 2010.

Questions and Answers

Q What do you think is your greatest talent?

A 'People tell me that one of the reasons why I succeeded was because I tend to close out everything else that goes on around me and concentrate on my race. I do not worry too much about things that go on in my life. I just train and run.'

Tirunesh Dibaba, www.tiruneshdibaba.net, 2011

Q After double Gold at the 2008 Olympics, did you think about retiring?

A 'Not at all. My ambition is to become Ethiopia's most successful Olympian. First of all, I want to win everything on the track that I can. Then it's the marathon!'

Tirunesh Dibaba, www.takethemagicstep.com, 2008

It's Dibaba herself, though, who has become the world's best. Her talent was obvious as soon as she stepped onto a track, but her ability to win races has developed over time. For a long time, Dibaba was losing races – she had the speed and ability to win, but she would start her sprint for the finish too soon, and run out of energy. Coaches focused on her race tactics, and the hard work has paid off. Dibaba is now the runner to beat.

Victoria Pendleton

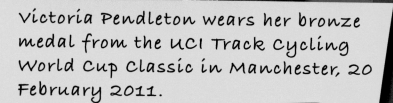

Victoria Pendleton wears her bronze medal from the UCI Track Cycling World Cup Classic in Manchester, 20 February 2011.

Victoria Pendleton has a tattoo on her right arm that says 'Today is the greatest day I've ever known'.

Stats!

Name: Victoria Louise Pendleton

Date of birth: 24 September 1980

Place of birth: Stotford, Bedfordshire, England

Sport: Track cycling

Teams: Team GB

Early days: Pendleton's dad was a former cycling champion, and first put her on a bike at the age of six. She grew up competing with her twin brother Alex, and was spotted by a national coach at just 16. Pendleton decided to put her education first, taking A-levels and then a degree in sports science. In her final year at university, she competed in the Commonwealth Games and turned professional as soon as she graduated.

Major achievements: Three gold medals at the 2007 World Championships for sprint, team sprint and Keirin (a mass sprint with 6-9 riders), a gold medal in the sprint at the Beijing Olympics in 2008 and a gold medal in the Keirin at the London Olympics in 2012. Pendleton has also won World Championship gold medals in 2005, 2008, 2009, 2010 and 2012. In 2013 she was awarded a CBE (Commander of the Order of the British Empire).

Secrets of success: Pendleton may not be as muscular as many track cyclists, but her strength-to-weight ratio is very high. She is light, powerful and aerodynamic in the saddle.

Life Story

When Victoria Pendleton was still in primary school, she went on long bike rides with her dad. But he wasn't doing it for 'father-daughter time' – the former champion would set the pace and Pendleton would have to struggle to keep up, or risk getting left behind. Sometimes she wanted to give up and go home but she kept cycling, built up her endurance and her perseverance has paid off.

Questions and Answers

Q **Did you always want to be a cyclist?**

A 'When I was a child and [people] asked me, "What do you want to be when you grow up?" I never knew. All I wanted to do was be really, really good at something!

Victoria Pendleton, *Observer Sports Monthly*, 2008

Q **Do you enjoy competing at the highest level?**

A 'I love riding my bike, getting out there and keeping fit. But racing is really tough because if I come second, people just ask: "What went wrong?" I came third at the World Cup and it was a disaster.'

Victoria Pendleton, the *Telegraph*, 2011

Pendleton takes the lead in the ladies sprint at the UCI Track Cycling World Cup Classic.

Pendleton delayed her professional cycling career until she had finished university. She then spent two intensive years at the World Cycling Centre in Switzerland, training every day. Her body was strong, but her mind was still unprepared. At the 2004 Olympics in Athens she went into the Games as favourite, but failed to win a medal.

She went back to the drawing board, spending time with the British team's psychologist and developed a mental attitude that turned her into a winner. Having won medals at the 2008 and 2012 Olympic Games, along with numerous World Championship medals, Pendleton retired from professional cycling in 2012.

Rafael Nadal

TENNIS SUPERSTAR

Nadal bites his trophy after beating Roger Federer of Switzerland in the men's final at the French Open in Paris, 5 June 2011.

Rafael Nadal is naturally right handed but was taught to play left handed because his coach believed his left arm was the stronger one!

Stats!

Name: Rafael Nadal Parera

Date of birth: 3 June 1986

Place of birth: Manacor, Majorca, Spain

Sport: Tennis

Teams: N/A

Early days: Nadal was introduced to tennis by his uncle, a former professional, at the age of three. At eight, he won a regional tournament for under-12s. By 12, he won the Spanish and European titles for his age group. At 15 he turned pro, and at 16 he reached the semi-finals of the boys' singles at Wimbledon. By 17 he had beaten Roger Federer for the first time, and was the youngest man to reach the third round at Wimbledon since Boris Becker.

Major achievements: Nadal has won 12 Grand Slam titles: Wimbledon (2008, 2010), US Open (2010), Australian Open (2009) and French Open (2005, 2006, 2007, 2008, 2010, 2011, 2012, 2013). He also won a gold medal at the Beijing Olympics in 2008.

Secrets of success: Nadal is known for his athleticism and speed around the court. His forehand shots are hit with an incredible amount of topspin – up to 4,900 revolutions per minute compared to an average 2,000 from players like Roger Federer.

Life Story

Nicknamed 'the King of Clay', and one of the sport's all-time greats, Rafael Nadal almost gave up tennis for good at 12 years old. He was a gifted footballer (his uncle Miguel played for Barcelona and Spain), and Nadal combined tennis and football quite happily. Two sports left little time for homework, however, so Nadal's father made him choose.

Although Uncle Miguel argued for football, Uncle Toni – Nadal's tennis coach since he was three – was more convincing and tennis won. Uncle Toni is still Nadal's coach today, and 12 Grand Slam victories later, no one doubts he made the right decision.

Nadal returns a shot during a quarterfinal match against Fernando Gonzalez of Chile at the US Open on 10 September 2009.

Nadal has had great success on the clay courts of the French Open, but more recently he has adapted his game and been successful on the hard courts of the Australian and US Opens, and the grass of Wimbledon. He is one of seven players to have won all four Grand Slams and the only player after Andre Agassi to win the Career Golden Slam – four Slams and an Olympic Gold. May his success continue for years to come!

Questions and Answers

Q What does success mean to you?

A 'Success isn't winning or losing. Success is being happy, enjoying practising, enjoying every day, and trying to be a better player than the day before.'

Rafael Nadal, *Sports Illustrated*, 2010

Q How do you motivate yourself after a defeat?

A 'In tennis, you have high moments and low moments... That's part of the sport. You have to accept the fantastic moments with the same calm as the problems. And tell yourself, hey, I'll come back and play my best tennis another day.'

Rafael Nadal, www.AustralianOpen.com, 2011

LeBron James

Basic Information
Born: Ohio, USA
Birthday: 30 December 1984
Sport: Basketball

Career

Background: James was introduced to basketball when he attended a $1 (60p) training class after school one day. He became the star performer at his high school, whose games were televised on ESPN and visited by National Basketball Association stars like Shaquille O'Neal.

Career highs: James was the 'first pick' in the 2003 NBA draft and spent seven years with the Cleveland Cavaliers. In 2010 he joined Miami Heat, helping the team to win the NBA Finals in 2013 and 2013. He has won two NBA Most Valuable Player awards, and gold medals at the 2008 and 2012 Olympics.

Career lows: James attracted widespread criticism and anger from fans when he left the Cleveland Cavaliers for Miami Heat in 2010.

Special skills: James is a leader on the court, not only scoring points, but providing multiple assists for teammates.

Shanaze Reade

Basic Information
Born: Crewe, UK
Birthday: 23 September 1988
Sport: BMX and track cycling

Career

Background: Reade began racing BMX at age 10, and bought her first BMX bike for just £1! By 17, she was competing professionally – against men as well as women – and winning. Her first race victory came in 2006, the same year she became British Number 1.

Career highs: After winning three World, eight European and five British championships, Reade recently moved on to track cycling. She took up the sport to keep fit for BMX, but won a gold medal in the women's team sprint at the 2007 World Championships with partner Victoria Pendleton.

Career lows: Reade entered the 2008 Olympics as favourite for Gold in the BMX but crashed in the final, and finished without a medal. She also missed out on a medal at the 2012 Olympics.

Special skills: A willingness to race through the pain barrier is essential for cycling. Reade has raced with broken bones in her foot, elbow and even spine.

Rory McIlroy

Basic Information
Born: County Down, Northern Ireland
Birthday: 4 May 1989
Sport: Golf

Career

Background: Rory picked up his first golf club at just 18 months old. He joined his local club at seven – the youngest ever member – and won the World Junior Championships in Florida at age nine.

Career highs: At 17, Rory was the number one ranked amateur player in the world. In 2007 he turned professional, and by 2009 he had won his first tournament. In 2011, Rory won the US Open by eight shots from his nearest rival, with an incredible total of 16 under par.

Career lows: Rory led the 2011 US Masters by four shots going into the final round, but hit an eight over par 80 to finish joint 15th.

Special skills: Rory is a very long hitter and has the concentration and drive to succeed.

Mahendra Singh Dhoni

Career

Background: Dhoni excelled in badminton and football at school. His football coach recommended him to the local cricket team where he quickly became first-choice wicketkeeper. He rose through the ranks, and made his debut for the Indian ODI (one-day international) team in 2004.

Career highs: His aggressive batting style has helped Dhoni break records. He scored 183 'not out' in 2005 against Sri Lanka, still a world record for the highest score in the second innings of an ODI. Promoted to captain, he won the 2007 World Twenty, and the 2011 Cricket World Cup, scoring an unbeaten 91 in the final and hitting a 6 to win the match!

Career lows: Scored two ducks (score of zero) in the 2007 World Cup, and 29 runs in the tournament.

Special skills: Dhoni's calm captaincy and powerful batting have taken India to number one in the world rankings.

Basic Information
Born: Jharkland, India
Birthday: 7 July 1981
Sport: Cricket

Wladimir Klitschko

Career

Background: Standing 6 foot 6.5inches (198cm) tall, Klitschko started boxing at school and in 1993 won the Junior European Championships. The following year he was second in the Junior World Championships. In 1996 he won a Gold medal in the Super-Heavyweight division at the Olympics.

Career highs: Klitschko won his first heavyweight title, the WBO belt, in 2000. He currently holds the WBA, IBF, IBO, WBO and Ring Magazine heavyweight titles. In July 2011, he defeated British boxer David Haye to win the WBA belt.

Career lows: Klitschko lost his WBO belt in 2003, when he was knocked out in just two rounds by Jamaican Corrie Sanders.

Special skills: One of the hardest punchers in heavyweight history, Klitschko uses a powerful left jab and a right cross to break down opponents.

Basic Information
Born: Semipalatinsk, Kazakhstan
Birthday: 25 March 1976
Sport: Heavyweight boxing

Natalie du Toit

Career

Background: Du Toit competed in the 1998 Commonwealth Games aged just 14. At 17 years old, she lost a leg when she was hit by a car on her way home from swimming practice. Three months later, before she could even walk again, she was back in the pool competing for a place in the 2002 Games.

Career highs: The South African won five Gold medals at the Paralympics in 2004 and 2008, and three Gold medals at the Commonwealth Games in 2010. She was also the first amputee ever to qualify for the Olympics, finishing 16th in the 10k marathon swim.

Career lows: Finished in 39th place in the 10km open water swim at the 2011 World Championships in Shanghai.

Special skills: Du Toit is recognised by her opponents for her incredible mental strength, as well as her physical endurance.

Basic Information
Born: Cape Town, South Africa
Birthday: 29 January 1984
Sport: Swimming

More champions to look out for

Tom Daley – UK diver
Missy Franklin – US swimmer
Abubaker Kaki Khamis – Sudanese runner
Peter Wilson – UK target shooter
Gemma Gibbons – UK judo
Lauren Mitchell – Australian gymnast
Grigor Dimitrov – Bulgarian tennis player
Neymar – Brazilian footballer
So Yeon Ryu – South Korean female golfer
Laura Robson – UK tennis player

Index